# Introduction

**Gustavo Facci's aerial picture of the statue**

## Christ the Redeemer

"In Him we have redemption through His blood, the forgiveness of our trespasses, according to the riches of His grace." – Ephesians 1:7

Particularly to those who harbor an inexplicable and irrational fear of heights, a trip to the pinnacle of Mount Corcovado is bound to rouse the kaleidoscope of butterflies in one's stomach, and at the very least, cover one's palms with a glistening film of sweat. A maximum of 345 passengers board the boxy, ribbon-red Trem do Corcovado. These modern, Swiss-made train carriages are perfectly safe, but the mechanical whirring and the rhythmic click-click-clicks as the train chugs up a set of sturdy tracks about 2.4-miles in length, to a summit that is 2,329-feet above ground, only adds to the suspense. But they say that what lies on the top of Corcovado makes the jarring trip up the mountain well worth its while, for this is none other than the home of the Cristo Redentor, one of the most famous statues in the world.

For just a fee of 43 Brazilian reals, which amounts to about $13, one is provided with a trip up to the peak and the privilege of taking a gander at the most renowned and spectacular landmark in all of Rio de Janeiro. The tram carriages are filled with the gorgeous harmonies of the samba band, paired with the beautiful beats of their tamborims and snare drums, and peppered with the non-stop shutter sounds from a variety of cameras. Those showing no signs of acrophobia peer out their windows, snapping away at the sweeping curtains of lush trees on either side of the tracks, and collectively breathe out in awe when the curtains opened up to a staggering, fog-kissed view of the city below from the edge of the towering mountain.

Visitors looking for an unforgettable hike are presented with the option of making the trek up to the peak on their own two feet. The Floresta da Tijuca, or the Tijuca National Forest, offers multiple winding, well-marked hiking trails that slither up the thick of what is said to be all that remains of the Atlantic rain forest that once blanketed the region. That being said, the 39 square-kilometer floresta now reigns as the largest "urban rain forest" in the world, packed with a vibrant spectrum of trees, shrubs, flowers, and greenery. From eucalyptus to mahogany and rosewood, it offers an enchanting collection of whispering creeks and gushing waterfalls, as well as swathes of rustic terrain.

On top of the nearly indistinguishable blend of natural and man-made features in the Tijuca tropical jungle, one might stroll past the Capela Mayrink, a quaint 19th-century chapel, and a treasury of caves and grottos, such as the Gruta Belmiro and the Gruta Paulo e Virgínia. The luckiest hikers – and at times, even some fortunate tram riders – might even come across one of the amusing creatures and critters that live in these parts, such as wild iguanas perched upon rocks,  marmosets and Capuchin monkeys swinging from branches, and even the rare Caracaras (a local falcon breed) or turkey vulture.

At the end of these trails, visitors will find a stone staircase consisting of 223 steps, leading up to a sturdy platform. Situated on this platform is a colossal statue fixed firmly upon a pedestal, none other than the Cristo Redentor, otherwise known as the legendary statue of Christ the Redeemer. The sea of tourists and visitors huddled together on the platform cock their heads back, their hands cupped over their eyes to shield themselves from the glare of the sun as they admire the century-old monument looming over them.

Others say this fabled monument is best appreciated after dark and from a distance, ideally from the crest of Sugar Loaf Mountain, the aptly-named loaf-shaped peak sitting opposite the Corcovado. Under the twinkling night sky, with Corcovado cloaked by layers of lingering fog, the glowing figure seems to float above the constellation of city lights, like the city's very own North Star, guiding and guarding over the maze of modern buildings and classic "shanty towns" of Rio de Janeiro.

But the Cristo Redentor is far more than just a princely statue or a tourist trap for urban explorers and adrenaline addicts. As one of the masterminds behind the statue once described the masterpiece, it is a "monument to science, art, and religion." Padre Omar, the rector of its chapel, called it "a religious symbol, a cultural symbol, and a symbol of Brazil." So significant and irreplaceable is the statue to the locals that modern artists continue to pay homage to the iconic landmark through graffiti art, elaborate murals, and intricately detailed sand sculptures on the Copacabana beach. Many of the Catholic Brazilian youth have also chosen to ink their skin with exquisite tattoos featuring the statue, from minimalist and standalone shoulder or arm pieces to massive chest and full back tattoos.

*Christ the Redeemer: The History and Legacy of the Western Hemisphere's Most Famous Christian Monument* chronicles the events leading up to the monument's conception, its construction, and the great architects and engineers behind the majestic monument. It also examines the legacy of this iconic Brazilian landmark. Along with pictures depicting important people, places, and events, you will learn about Christ the Redeemer like never before.

Christ the Redeemer: The History and Legacy of the Western Hemisphere's Most Famous Christian Monument

About Charles River Editors

Introduction

Conception

Design

Construction

History

Online Resources

Further Reading

Free Books by Charles River Editors

Discounted Books by Charles River Editors

## Conception

"But that which cannot be bought with gold does not take its value from gold. The best way to use the gold of the Redeemer is for the redemption of those in peril." – attributed to St. Ambrose, 4th century Bishop of Milan

For a deeper dive into why the locals hold the monument in such high regard, one must first unearth its religious roots. Ever since the Portuguese colonists set soil on the land and planted the seeds of Catholicism in the 16th century, the faith has only experienced exponential growth. According to a religion-based census conducted in Brazil in 1890, an astounding 14,179,615 residents registered as Catholics, followed by just 143,743 Protestants, 7,257 non-religious folk, and 3,300 who bowed before a different deity, making roughly 98.9% of the population Catholic. By the 1940s, that number had climbed to an even 99%.

The Portuguese conquerors who anchored their vessels along the golden Bahian shores of Rio Buranhém (approximately 646 miles north of Rio de Janeiro) in April of 1500 had unwittingly wandered into a tropical paradise, inhabited by an "exotic" array of native tribes and a wealth of natural riches. This was only intended as a stopover en route to India, but as soon as Commander Pedro Alvares Cabral, who captained the expedition, ventured further into the land and dug deeper into its pulsating promise and potential, it made less and less sense for the Portuguese crown to pass up on such a gem of a discovery. After scouting out the land for a little over a week, Cabral drew up a report of his findings, loaded a selection of foreign timber onto the vessels, and sailed back to the motherland to unveil these discoveries to the king.

**A painting depicting Cabral sighting Brazil in 1500**

To start with, the place was bristling with pau-brasil, or "Brazilwood," which were large, shrub-like trees ornamented with yellow flowers tinged with reds and oranges. The wood derived from these trees, which inspired the name of the "newly discovered" terrain, was used to carve out bows for various stringed instruments, and the creamy red dye extracted from it was ideal for the production of textile dyes. The endless stretches of fertile land would later be converted into fields for sugar plantations, which would soon become the "agricultural and financial pillar of Brazil."

**A Brazilwood tree**

Agricultural nirvana aside, Brazil also hosted plenty of untapped deposits of gold and other minerals. Best of all, observed the Portuguese explorers, the Brazilian natives – or "infidels," as they were derogatorily referred to – were primitive, pitifully armed, and trusting, which not only meant that their minds were begging to be molded, they would be easy to "handle."

Like many natives who were robbed by conquest-hungry European adventurers of their lands, the Brazilian natives made the mistake of lowering their guards and entertaining the deceptively friendly Portuguese explorers. Tribesmen shuffled forth and gifted them with peace offerings of ravishing headdresses fashioned out of parrot feathers, and they nourished their visitors with plenty of food and drink. During their 9-day stay, the Portuguese managed to earn and deepen their trust by exposing them to and sharing with some of them the iron-made tools and weapons they had brought along from Europe. Cabral even tested their reactions to and tolerance of foreign spiritual concepts and religions by inviting them to observe a traditional Catholic mass service. While they seemed to be more curious than moved by what to them were alien spiritual rites, the Portuguese took this as a sign that once properly indoctrinated with the word of God, they would be quick to change their ways.

It was only in 1549 that esteemed soldier and nobleman Tomé de Sousa first arrived in Brazil. As the first governor general of the Colonial Brazil, de Sousa installed the first Portuguese nerve center in Salvador, or as it was formerly known, "Bahia." This would remain the capital of the Portuguese colonies until it was moved to Rio de Janeiro in the mid-18th century.

**De Sousa**

Among the colonists who arrived with de Sousa were members from the newly established Jesuit order. Rather than opening up the indigenous Brazilians to Catholicism and peacefully inviting them into their new faith, blinded by their desire to rectify the damned souls of the infidels, the Jesuit and Catholic Iberian missionaries outlawed the original customs, traditions, and beliefs that existed in the lands long before them. As could be expected, the natives began to resist, but their outdated weapons were no match for the colonists, and as such, they were rendered helpless as the Portuguese destroyed almost every last trace of their cultural and religious jewels.

In addition to the forced conversions, the Portuguese missionaries enforced their own version of the Inquisition, targeting and persecuting any natives or Portuguese settlers who dared to defy the Catholic Church. As time progressed, Catholicism, as well as elements from Portuguese customs, became more and more infused, until it eventually dominated the local culture. The Christian population of Brazil only continued to blossom from there, especially in the 19th century, when the Iberian and Brazilian Roman Catholics were joined by a surge of Italian, Polish, and German Catholic immigrants.

Included in the exuberant report delivered by Cabral to King Manuel I of Portugal and the Algarves was an encapsulation of one granite mountain with a distinctive, slightly skewed peak, sitting in the heart of what is present-day Rio de Janeiro in southeastern Brazil. The first batch of Portuguese explorers to hike up to the summit of the granite peak named it the "Pináculo da Tentação," or in English, the "Pinnacle of Temptation." The name stems from the Biblical stories found in the Books of Matthew, Mark, and Luke chronicling Satan's attempts to tempt Jesus, in one instance urging him to leap from the highest peak in the land. About a century later, the mountain was rechristened the "Corcovado" for its shape, obtained from the Portuguese term "uma corcund," which translates into "hunchback."

**King Manuel I of Portugal**

**Beck Stei's picture of Corcovado**

On September 7, 1822, Brazil entered a historic new chapter when it triumphantly declared its independence from Portugal. On the 12th of October, Dom Pedro I was crowned the first Emperor of Brazil, and a "representative parliamentary constitutional monarchy" was set in place. The freshly instated Império do Brasil (the Empire of Brazil), composed of territories both in modern-day Brazil and Uruguay, was enormous, and while rather lacking in residents for a land of such a size, it was colored by different ethnicities.

**Pedro I**

**Maria Leopoldina**

It was two years later that Dom Pedro I ordered a band of lumberjacks to clear a path to the crown of the Corcovado. Once the path was completed, the emperor, accompanied by his consort, the lovely Empress Maria Leopoldina, traveled to the summit of Corcovado, and they were immediately taken with the invigorating fresh air and fantastic view of the city below them, not to mention the stunning native flora and fauna they chanced across along the way.

Following behind the couple was Maria Graham, the daughter of a British naval officer and a proficient globetrotter who was not only a close acquaintance of the empress but would briefly serve as the governess to their daughter, Princess Doña Maria de Gloria. That same year, she published *Journal of a Voyage to Brazil,* a memoir she authored and illustrated that documented the brilliant natural and artificial features of the land through watercolor sketches and drawings of the sights, including that of the beauty on Mount Corcovado. As Gray Bell, author of the *Beautiful Rio de Janeiro*, published in 1914, put it, "To go to Rio de Janeiro and not go up Corcovado is a folly."

The Catholic Church would not fall under the Corcovado's spell until 1853, when an intrigued priest by the name of Pedro Maria Boss and a company of friends journeyed up to the peak of the mountain. There, the French-born Catholic priest, like those who came before him, became entranced by the striking vegetation and colorful creatures living in these parts, so much so that he began to envision a commemorative structure of some sort to embellish this pristine mountaintop.

Father Boss mulled over a few concepts until he finally settled upon one fit for a proposal 6 years later. In the summer of 1859, a bright-eyed Father Boss approached the 13-year-old Dona Isabel, Princess Imperial, heiress presumptive, and eldest daughter of then Dom Pedro II, and presented to her his proposal. This monument, which he styled the "Cristo Redentor," was to be erected on the summit of the delightfully wooded Corcovado. While it would be chiseled to resemble their Savior, Father Boss sweetened the potential project by promising to construct it in her honor. To Boss' disappointment, the young princess appeared anything but impressed, and though she politely assured him that she would consider it, it was clear that the reportedly humble and devout God-fearing princess had no intention of carrying out the request. When Dom Pedro II returned home from the Paraguayan War in 1870, Father Boss' proposal continued to collect dust, until the disheartened priest finally accepted that his vision would never come to fruition, at least not in his lifetime.

**Isabel**

**Pedro II of Brazil**

As regent of the empire, Isabel proved to be an open-minded and competent head of state, even using her position to abolish the horrific institution of slavery, but her leadership, largely due to her gender, would be questioned time and again. Though she was strong-willed, yet cautious and flexible, she was impervious to the influence of aggressive politicians, even as her critics accused her of being no more than a puppet for either the Catholic Church or the French crown on behalf of her husband, Gaston of Orléans. Bearing this in mind, historians believe Isabel's reluctance towards the construction of the statue was built on the fear that her detractors would use it as ammunition to further mar her character. Those who scoffed at the prospect of a princess regnant labeled her "feeble-minded" and "easily impressionable," with an "inherent inability" to handle budgets and administer policies. As such, accepting what they were certain to deem a vanity project would give them an excuse to condemn her for squandering state funds. Furthermore, such a project would only distract her from what would be her crowning achievement: the publishing and enforcement of the *Lei Áurea,* or "Golden Law," which effectively extinguished slavery in Brazil in 1888. She referred to slavery as a "repugnant...attack against human freedom."

The dismay of Father Boss, who eventually passed away before the idea of the statue was revived, was ultimately immortalized in a poem he penned for the prologue of the 1903 edition of Imitation of Christ.

"Oh Corcovado:

There rises the stone giant, clinging to it, towering and sad, as if questioning the immense horizon –

'When will it come? For so many centuries I have waited

Yes, here is the only pedestal in the world...'

Wake up quickly, lift up the image of Jesus the Savior on that sublime peak..."

**A 19<sup>th</sup> century picture of Corcovado**

As it turns out, it would take a series of drastic developments that threatened the fabric of the nation's godliness for Boss' project to be resurrected.

The successful military coup in mid-November of 1889, which saw the abrupt deposition of the second and last emperor of Brazil, Dom Pedro II, gave rise to the Brazilian Republic. The "provisional government" of the new Republican regime continued to uphold the national constitution published 8 years prior, which aimed to permanently sever ties between the Church and the State. As per the stipulations of the decree, all Brazilian citizens were guaranteed freedom of religion. Any public officers or figures who attempted to obstruct or disrupt the "formation of religious societies" would be duly punished. With the role of the Catholic Church now dramatically reduced, making it no more important or influential than the other budding new and foreign religions in Brazil, Father Boss' project appeared to have been forgotten for good.

Although the Catholic Church had initially championed the idea of an independent Brazil as early as 7 decades before the military mutiny, Catholics had always railed against retiring the parliamentary-based constitutional monarchy in favor of a republican-style form of ruling, the latter a trend picking up amongst ex-Spanish American colonies. Up until the sudden political transition, the emperors solicited annual taxes from the people at the behest of the Catholic Church. And though the Church, in accordance with the covenant sealed between the Brazilian crown and the Catholic clerics, agreed not to interfere with certain political affairs, such as commercial policies pertaining to the local industries and so forth, they governed over the state's educational and matrimonial sectors and superintended its burial grounds.

Following the divorce of Church and State, the yearly tithes the Catholic Church had been so reliant on were promptly terminated. Likewise, the Catholic Church, or any other faith, for that matter, would no longer receive any financial support from the federal government. Those whose livelihoods hinged on the Church would be awarded their salaries for the following year, but they had to search for other avenues of income after that. Moreover, the Catholic Church was no longer vested with the power to register births, marriages, and deaths. All Christian topics were also removed from the public school curricula.

The Catholic Church, however, was granted the right to govern itself, and it continued to hold dominion over their own churches, headquarters, and religious centers, as well as its own power structures and treasuries. The Church bore the right to claim squares of burial grounds that would be reserved for the Catholics, but the Church had to abide by the laws and regulations set in place by the Republican government. Church authorities sunk deeper into despair when the government formally erased all religious holidays and Catholic-related memorial days, barring the Christian Sabbath, from the state calendar, and replaced them with 9 secular holidays. The teeth-grinding only worsened when the government, following the examples of the United States and France, approved a law that legalized civil marriages, as well as divorces.

The discontent of the Catholics would soon prove to be the least of the state's problems. The federal republic was now governed by the joint oligarchies of São Paulo and Minas Gerais. The presidents of the oligarchies, who ruled in turn, strove to reinforce their power and assert their dominance over their subjects through a spoils system (also known as a "patronage system"), meaning their cabinets were staffed with those that had been instrumental in securing their wins. As a result, most of the high-ranking officials were inexperienced and severely deficient in the knowledge needed to properly execute their duties, leading to further internal dissension, as well as the dissatisfaction of the masses.

The introduction of industrialization and urbanization to Brazilian cities resulted in an overall increase in productivity and efficiency, but like every upside, it was evened out by the resentment of the growing number of unemployed farmers and low-skilled laborers. And while the influx of European immigrants occasioned the advent of the middle class, the unemployed – the majority of them former Afro-Brazilian slaves – and those trapped in the echelon below it found it progressively difficult to make ends meet. Unsurprisingly, the nation experienced an upswing in crime.

In late June of 1914, a 20-year-old Serbian nationalist, Gavrilo Princip, fired into the black open-top convertible rolling down one of the streets of Sarajevo, killing Archduke Franz Ferdinand of Austria and triggering World War I. For the first few years of the war, Brazil's 9th president, Venceslau Brás, wisely declared a policy of neutrality, opting to keep Brazil out of the conflict. Instead, the government chose to direct efforts towards bolstering relations with Chile and Argentina through the ABC (Argentina-Brazil-Chile) pact of 1915. Still, as the multi-ethnic Brazilian residents watched the war unfold from the sidelines, they began to split up into separate camps of opinion. The bulk of the masses sided with Allies, leading to "nationalistic societies" springing up all over Brazil, whereas a fraction of them (predominantly the German-Brazilians) staunchly stood with the Central Powers.

**Brás**

Although Brazil had hoped to wash its hands of the convoluted conflict, Brazilians were feeling the impact of war through a faltering economy. Not only were more and more ports around the world being blockaded – most notably, the United Kingdom, one of the largest buyers of the local coffee – their supply of imported oil was running dangerously low. But when a number of Brazilian merchant vessels were ambushed and sunk by German submarines and warships between mid-1916 and early 1917, the enemy ships unabashedly flouting the laws regarding neutral states, an infuriated President Brás declared war against the Central Powers. The protests of the Catholic Church fell on deaf ears.

While Brazil suffered a significantly smaller death toll in comparison to the approximately 8.3 million soldiers (casualties from opposing parties combined) killed throughout the course of the Great War, the masses were traumatized by the events, and they continued to remain restless when faced with the crippling repercussions of a world war. Less than half a year before the war came to a close, "libertarian militants" founded the Rio de Janeiro Anarchist Alliance, which aimed to overthrow the oligarchic republic and install new councils comprising deserving and fairly-appointed politicians with working class and military backgrounds.

In the months of June and July 1919, major streets and public squares were hijacked by protesters staging strike after strike. These picketers, which included dockers, marble-makers, textile workers, carpenters, and so on, cried for shorter and more reasonable working hours, as well as higher wages to combat the rocketing costs of living. For several weeks on end, pandemonium ensued throughout the city streets, which eventually became unnecessarily painted with the blood of both protesters and police officers alike. Many storefronts shuttered their windows and double-bolted their doors, but even then, unruly protesters laid waste to these innocent establishments in fits of rage.

The dominoes of misfortune only continued to tumble. In September of that year, the 1918 Spanish Flu Pandemic breached the Brazilian border. By the end of the next month, tens of thousands exposed to the virus had died. Some 15,000 would perish in Rio de Janiero alone; another 600,000, about 66% of the population, were bedridden. To put this tragedy into perspective, 930 of the 1,073 deaths that occurred on the 22nd of October alone are said to have been victims of the outbreak. Many conservative Church authorities reckoned the disease was a direct punishment for straying further and further away from God's light.

In addition to all the civil commotion and political rivalries, Brazilians, the Church insisted, were engaging in immoral and hedonistic practices. The parks in Rio de Janeiro's entertainment districts, particularly in Constitution Square, they claimed, which housed honorable statues dedicated to the past emperors, were being "desecrated" by the growing presence of homosexual couples unafraid to show their affection for each other. Something had to be done to put an end to this "godlessness" running rampant across their beloved Catholic nation.

### Design

"Come to me, all who labor and are heavy laden, and I will give you rest."
– Matthew 11:25-28

At the dawn of the 20th century, the demoralized Catholic Church in Brazil became more desperate than ever to tighten its loosening grip on the masses, for many of them were jumping aboard the Protestant ship, and others were converting to Islam. The movement that intended to breathe new life into the Brazilian Catholic Church was largely spearheaded by Sebastião Leme da Silveira Cintra, a Brazilian-born cardinal and the future Archbishop of São Sebastião do Rio de Janeiro. In March of 1921, Cintra was appointed the Coadjutor Archbishop of the Brazilian capital, upon the news of the irreversibly deteriorating health of Joaquim Arcoverde de Albuquerque Cavalcanti (or Arcoverde, for short), the republic's first cardinal. Now that he was officially the successor to Arcoverde's coveted title, Cintra, as his second-in-command, was expected to assist the cardinal in overseeing the See of Rio de Janeiro.

**Cintra**

In order to rebrand the Church and hopefully recoup and entice both old and new converts, Cintra decided that a reorganization of the hierarchy was in order. In an effort to consolidate the Church's power, rid the system of the dead weight, and ultimately rehabilitate a tarnished reputation, the Coadjutor Archbishop established the National Eucharistic Congress. These congresses, first conceptualized by French Bishop Louis Gaston de Ségur in early 1881, were conferences attended by laity and ecclesiastics of all ranks "for the purpose of celebrating and glorifying the Holy Eucharist...[by bearing] witness to the Real Presence of Jesus in the Eucharist...and [by] seeking the best means to spread its knowledge and love throughout the world."

Religious motivations aside, these national open-air Masses and ceremonies, which typically lasted several days, was an opportunity for Brazilians of all races, classes, and backgrounds to befriend one another, further cementing a sense of unity within the Catholic Church.

It seemed as if Cintra's campaign to restore the prestige of the Church was gaining some traction. Shortly thereafter, the pistol-toting, but prayerful Lieutenant Pedro Carolino Pinto de Almeida, chief of the guards that stood watch of the Ministry of Finance building, decided to contribute in the name of the lay public. Rounding up a small guild of like-minded laymen based in Rio de Janeiro, he created the Círculo Católico, or the "Catholic Circle." In the weeks that followed, the circle brainstormed on how to best boost the morale of their Christian brethren. Some suggested a newspaper or magazine of some sorts to propagate their cause, but this idea was quickly rejected, for their fledgling paper would soon disappear into the torrents of publications already in circulation. Others tentatively proposed the staging of additional rallies, but this too, would be shot down, as mass gatherings organized by inexperienced orchestrators were far more prone to tumult and disorder.

Then came a suggestion from another member, presumably a former clerk of the Catholic Church or an acquaintance of the deceased Father Boss. This member mused about the possibility of attempting to revive the proposal the Princess Imperial had spurned decades ago. Their success, he added, would be far more probable, as it would be presented to a brand new pair of eyes, to say nothing of the current climate of the Church. Such a grand and blatantly visible monument would not only come just in time for the centenary of the nation's political independence, it would certainly help in reinstating the prominence and credibility of the Catholic Church.

Once the Catholic Circle had settled upon Boss' proposal, a committee was dispatched to the streets so that they could spread word to and gauge the interest of the public. To their relief, the project was greeted with resounding support. In 1922 alone, local author Laurita Lacerda managed to procure over 20,000 signatures – mostly from women – for a petition addressed to President Epitácio Pessoa requesting the construction of the Cristo Redentor.

**Pessoa**

Despite such an impressive feat, little is known about Laurita Lacerda. Some sources describe her as a spunky and strong-minded feminist, known to have been a regular contributor to *Revista Feminina* ("The Feminine Magazine"), a women's rights publication founded by Virgilina de Souza Salles that made its rounds until 1936. As the *Revista Feminina* was geared towards a "traditional" Catholic female audience, its articles are noted to have been themed with subjects that many would consider narrow-minded and anti-feminist in this day and age. Examples of weekly columns included "Fashion," "My Husband's Menu," and "How to Decorate My Home," among many others.

Incapable of ignoring the emphatic support behind the nearly 70 year old proposal, President Pessoa approved its construction, but not without some hesitation. Pessoa's approval ratings remained consistently elevated for a reason – his people lauded him as a rational, equitable, and open-minded president. Not only had he funded the establishment of the University of Rio de Janeiro, he brought the first radio station to Brazil, and would authorize the construction of over 200 dams in Northeast Brazil throughout his career. He earned more favor with the public when he appointed a civilian, respected historian Pandiá Calógeras, the Minister of War. Pessoa had never publicly aligned himself with any one faith and was an advocate of freedom of worship, but he worried about the backlash he was bound to receive from other religious communities all the same. Still, at the end of the day, Pessoa, a firm believer of the majority rule, realized it would make even less sense to alienate what was still the largest chunk of the population by far.

Just as Pessoa predicted, his office was flooded with complaints from the Protestant and Muslim communities, therefore delaying the start of construction for some time. The displeased bitterly criticized Pessoa and his government for disobeying the constitution and displaying undue favor to the Catholics. The late March 1923 edition of the *Jornal Batista*, the official newspaper of the Brazilian Baptist community, went as far as to call the monument in question "an affront to God."

The Protestants argued against the use of crucifixes and any other representations of the Lord, for it went against their interpretation of the 2nd Commandment: "Thou shalt not make unto thee any graven image, or any likeness of any thing that is in heaven above, or that is in the earth beneath, or that is in the water under the earth..." The worship of such images, they asserted, would only lead to idolatry, diverting the attention and reverence away from God and Christ and towards these "graven images" instead. The Brazilian Jewish community also expressed their distaste for the monument, as they believed there was no creation on earth that could "adequately stand in for God."

Expecting these adverse reactions, President Pessoa dismissed their complaints, and he simply assured the aggrieved parties that if they had approached him first with a project of such magnitude, they, too, would have received a stamp of approval.

At this point, a location had to be chosen for the home of the Christ the Redeemer monument. For this, the Catholic Circle reached out to the masses with a public poll. After much deliberation and debate, the choices were narrowed down to the following three settings: the picturesque hilltop of the Santo Antônio do Monte in what is now the state of Minas Gerais; Sugar Loaf Mountain, which sits on a peninsula by Guanabara Bay; and the "hunchbacked" Mount Corcovado, the original location of the failed project. Corcovado won by a landslide.

In September 1923, the archdiocese of Rio de Janeiro, with much assistance from the Catholic Circle, kicked off the Semana do Monumento, or in English, "Monument Week." As its name implies, the week-long event was dedicated to raising funds and collecting even more signatures for the Cristo Redentor, for it was solely up to them to finance the ambitious project. Citizens later recounted the extraordinary effort applied to the event by its organizers. Volunteers of all ages, most of them women, posted themselves on every street corner, armed with donation buckets, jars, and other receptacles, as well as bells and signs explaining their cause. Younger volunteers loitered underneath the apartments and homes in affluent neighborhoods with open sheets, catching the coins that tenants and homeowners tossed out of their windows.

Needless to say, almost all of the 100,000 réis they raked in through donations came from Brazilian Catholics, topped off with a smattering of spare change from those not affiliated with any faiths but who wished to witness the execution of this grandiose monument they were promised. João Havelange, the 7th President of the Fédération Internationale de Football Association (FIFA), is said to have been part of a "scout group" that worked the streets during the Semana do Monumento.

When the Cristo Redentor's critics caught wind of the whopping amount the Catholic Church had managed to raise in a span of just seven days, they again began to belittle and deprecate the monument. "What Christ is one that asks His people for alms?" the headlines of the time demanded. Local politician Adolfo Bergamini, who belonged to the Protestant faith, mockingly posed this question to his "coreligionists": "An avalanche of girls, women, and men come to the street with a bag in hand to beg. Have they transformed the population of Rio into a true Christ?"

Rather than humor or fight back against the critics who were clearly baiting them into a dispute to stall for more time, the Catholic Church chose to rise above the opposition and carried on with the preparations for the project. By the end of February 1922, more than a year before Monument Week, the judges of the design competition for the Christ the Redeemer statue had already chosen its winner: a native 50-year-old civil engineer by the name of Heitor de Silva Costa. Apart from his obvious talents, Silva Costa, born in the Brazilian capital to Eleia Guimaraes and Dr. Jose de Silva Costa, seemed to be destined for the job. Having been raised in a well-to-do family, the young boy was privileged enough to be exposed to the finest education available only to the upcoming generation of society's elites. After the completion of his "classical studies" at Abilio College in 1886, he moved onto an engineering school in São Pedro de Alcântra, where he received exceptional grades and multiple commendations from his professors. Following up on his potential, Heitor enrolled himself at the Polytechnic University of Rio de Janeiro, to hone his technical skills. But he was not just an engineering prodigy – he, too, was gifted with a creative eye, as seen in the slew of structures and statues he would design and help materialize, including the Neogothic Cathedral of St. Peter of Alcantara and the throne of Saint Fatima in Petrópolis, the "Imperial City" of Brazil.

**Halley Pacheco de Oliveira's picture of a bust of Heitor**

Even when Heitor trekked up to the top of Mount Corcovado to survey the site of the monument, he was well aware of what it meant to take on this immense undertaking. "Making an image of Christ is a high aspiration and a big responsibility," Heitor scribbled in his journal. "Making it in huge proportions would be, without a doubt, the greatest aspiration and responsibility of one's life."

Heitor's first sketches featured a bronze monument (as Father Boss had intended) that would face the rising sun. Another excerpt lifted from his journal explains his decision: "The statue of the divine savior shall be the first image to emerge from obscurity in which the earth is plunged, and to receive the salute of the star of the day which, after surrounding it with its radiant luminosity, shall build at sunset around its head a halo fit for the Man-God."

The Redeemer himself, depicted in a loose-fitting robe with his chiseled chest bulging out of his open V-neck, held a massive cross against him with one hand and carried a small globe in his palm with the other. Though it was this take on the Redeemer that won the popular vote of the public, other engineers and sculptors ridiculed him for the cumbersome design. Others who thought it too hokey for their tastes nicknamed it "Christ with a Ball."

Heitor's ego was understandably wounded, but when it dawned on him that the cross and globe-wielding Christ the Redeemer was, in fact, much too technically challenging of a design, and one that was only certain to bring about endless headaches, he made his way back to the drawing board. Heitor worked on a new design for weeks, but when he failed to conjure up his creative juices, he waded through the mass of balled up papers on his floors and headed into town to find his muse.

The engineer climbed up to the rooftops of multistory buildings in all corners of the city for a better view of the Corcovado. At some point, his roaming eyes became riveted to the latticed structure of a 131-foot radio transmission tower installed by the American Westinghouse Electric Corporation. These contraptions, shaped like miniature Eiffel Towers, came with horizontal arm-like supports of equal length jutting out from its top and center. It was then that he decided that the silhouette of the new monument would be built in the shape of a cross.

While the idea of a cross-shaped structure was anything but new, a cross-shaped monument of such a size had yet to be tackled. Heitor made a beeline for the nearest library, where he consulted texts from any classical architect who had dabbled in the subject, going as far back to works published by Ancient Greek engineers. Notwithstanding their lack of tools and technology, they possessed a remarkable understanding of proportion and scale when it came to design. Heitor also leafed through the works of Leonardo da Vinci, focusing on the "sacred geometry of the Vitruvian Man."

Hoping that an extra set of eyes would prevent him from making any more mistakes on the design, be they careless or crucial, he traveled to Italy, where he contacted Florentine artist Carlos Oswald. There, Heitor presented to Oswald a simplified design of Christ with outstretched arms, making the Redeemer Himself the cross, meant to symbolize "the redemption of mankind at the crucifixion." Once the pair had completed the necessary tweaks, it was concluded that for maximum impact, the mammoth structure would have to be visible from the city center from as far as 2.5 miles (4 kilometers) away. With that established, the monument needed to be extremely resilient and so sturdy that the main frame would be able to support its arms, thereby ensuring that the immovable structure would remain upright even when confronted with the worst storms and earthquakes.

With that, in the spring of 1924, Heitor set off for France, home of Albert Caquot, supposedly the "best living French engineer" at the time. Caquot first earned his celebrity through his invention of a "stabilized captive balloon," which provided the French forces with an edge when conducting aerial observations on their enemies during the First World War. The eminent engineer, who made his bread and butter as a professor of mechanical science in 3 of the top engineering schools in Paris, was also the first to utilize reinforced concrete when commissioned to build an assortment of over 300 dams and bridges in France, such as the Madeleine and Lafayette Bridges, and the La Girotte Dam. There were few who could rival his prowess for sleek, but practical designs and accurate calculations. But it would be Caquot's design of the Cristo Redentor's internal structure that propelled him to fame on an international stage.

## Caquot (front and center)

It did not take long for Heitor to get on board with the idea of using reinforced concrete as both the foundation and the internal structure of the monument. It was one of the most recent innovations of the era, and it was embraced by any architect and engineer worth their salt. Besides, metal frameworks constructed out of the traditional materials of cast iron or copper were susceptible to corrosion – particularly with acid rain – and was bound to become brittle over time. Heitor elaborated on his decision in his journal, writing, "The public is used to seeing reinforced concrete in engineering work, pillars, columns, etc., but I presented it as being able to serve for a work of art; it still seems unusual. However, this material is modern, and the material of the future..."

## Construction

"There's some task which the God of all the universe, the Great Creator, your redeemer in Jesus Christ has for you to do, and which will remain undone until by faith and obedience you step into the will of God." – Alan Redpath, 20th century British evangelist

Heitor circuited Paris, Florence, Rome, Munich, and other European cities to assemble his dream team of engineers, sculptors, and builders, interviewing prospective candidates and riffling through résumés, but it was in the City of Lights that he found most of his talents. Shortly after his fruitful meeting with Caquot, Heitor was approached by the prolific French sculptor Antoine Bourdelle, a protégé of the great Auguste Rodin, best known for his gilt bronze bust of Gustave Eiffel and his ornate, life-sized monumental sculptures of famous figures from Greek mythology. Bourdelle escorted Heitor around his workshops, and offered to produce for him a model roughly 13 feet (4 meters) in size.

**Bourdelle**

As impressed as Heitor was by Bourdelle's work, the Brazilian engineer ultimately elected to work with another one of his most fierce competitors, French-Polish sculptor Paul Landowski, instead. Even as a young lad, Landowski showed a flair for art and seemed to have an instinctive handle on clay. He made one of his first sculptures, of Saint Blandine, when he was no older than 13, which he baked in the wood-fired bread oven of the Chézy-sur-Marne, a local bakery where he worked as an assistant baker after school and during the holidays. A fast and avid learner, the young boy devoured art history textbooks and classical literature, sharpening his sculpting skills and fishing for inspiration.

**Landowski**

In 1906, the 31-year-old Landowski rented out a small house in Boulogne-sur-Seine and converted his ground floor to a studio. Landowski was more than familiar with incorporating the themes of "heroism" and the "race for glory" into his pieces. When the First World War ended, Landowski received an inundation of commissions for monuments devoted to fallen soldiers and other casualties of the war. Though he found some of his creativity hampered by the restrictions imposed upon him by his clients, he was given a chance to build what would soon turn out to be a glowing portfolio, which included works such as the Victory Monument in Casablanca and the Monument to the Dead of Algiers. What he hoped would be his magnum opus, however, was Le Temple de l'homme, or in English, the "Temple of Man." This magnificent temple, he insisted, would embody "the glory of man, with all his battles and victories."

By the time Heitor was making overtures to Landowski, the Parisian sculptor was no longer a struggling artist and could afford to pass up on projects that failed to pique his interest. Even so, Heitor, promising Landowski creative freedom and an appetizing paycheck, managed to convince him to put the construction of Le Temple de l'homme on hold to take on the order. Landowski, dazzled by Heitor's persistence and intrigued by the "voguishly art deco" style of Oswald's sketches, agreed to contribute, taking this as an extension of his "Temple of Man" project.

Between the 27th of May and the 20th of July in 1924, the duo conferred with one another about the technical details behind the Cristo Redentor.

Landowski was tasked with fashioning a 13 foot model of the statue out of clay and creating the molds for the head and hands of Christ the Redeemer. Heitor explained to him that the head and hands were to be constructed with artistic appeal in mind. As for the body and arms, Heitor was more concerned about its durability and the soundness of its structure than he was about its aesthetics. A finalized order was signed on the 3rd of November.

Judging by the multiple letters the pair exchanged throughout the course of their collaboration, it certainly seemed as if they worked well together. "Your process was certainly excellent," Landowski gushed to Heitor in one of his letters. "Mathematics shall always be the queen of architecture, and even of sculpture." The admiration appeared to be requited. Landowski gloated to his wife in one of his letters to her: "Da Silva is very happy with my sketch of Christ."

Landowski started his process by designing a series of models in varying heights and charging his apprentices with creating these sculptures based on his diagrams. Using a model of approximately 7.5 feet, he was able to guesstimate the size and positioning of the body and the head. He then tinkered with a larger model of 8.9 feet, perfecting the dimensions, proportions, and other minor details before moving on to the 13 foot model. It was through these trials and errors that Landowski was able to make the following observation: "The more one enlarges a statue, the more it is necessary to reduce the size of its head. The average adult is about 7.5 heads (a term used in modern figure drawing to indicate the distance from the top of one's head to one's chin). Life-size monuments are normally 8.2 or 9.2 heads tall. Therefore, my Christ of Rio must be, at the very least, 12 heads tall. Otherwise, the figure appears short."

Once the dimensions were finalized, Landowski refined Oswald's drawings, updating his old-fashioned art deco designs by smoothing down the hard edges of the Redeemer's jaw and facial features and rounding the tips of his fingers for more realism. Landowski's mentees then began work on the molds for the "real size" head, as well as one for Christ's hands. One of Landowski's students later claimed that her hands had been selected for the molds, and it was only as she lay on her deathbed that she finally admitted that her story was fictitious.

Regardless, once the clay had hardened, the head and hands were removed from their molds, and a glaze of soapstone triangles meticulously glued onto its surface. He had arranged a few test runs the previous week at the Gentil and Bourdet Factory, a ceramic and furniture manufacturing company famed for its mosaic work, to outline the placement of the tiles for maximum effect. The completed products were then carefully loaded into the back of cargo vessels destined for Rio de Janeiro.

The material of the monument's finish was the cause of many sleepless nights. In the weeks leading up to his final decision, Heitor, who had whipped up a list of potential materials that would cover the "rough and crude" exterior of the concrete statue, became increasingly exasperated the closer he inched towards the end of his list. "We were marching towards the inevitable artistic failure, without being able to go back," reads a line from one of his journal entries at the time.

Once again, it would take a dose of fresh air and a stroll around fresh, unfamiliar surroundings to unclog his creative block. After closing up shop one evening, Heitor decided to take an alternative route to his inn and headed for the Champs Elysees. There, he became captivated by a beautiful babbling fountain towards the end of the avenue, its facade coated with a mosaic composed of glittering silver shards. Heitor was ecstatic. He rushed home and jotted down in his journal, "By seeing how the small tiles covered all the curved profiles of the fountain, I was soon taken by the idea of using them on the image which I always had in my thoughts...Moving from the concept to the making of it took less than 24 hours. The next morning, I went to a ceramic studio where I made the first samples."

Heitor was relieved to have finally found his winner, though he was mildly irritated that he had not thought of it sooner. Soapstone was first popularized by the 18$^{th}$ century sculptor Antonio Francisco Lisboa, better known as "Aleijadinho the Cripple," based in Minas Gerais. As the story goes, Aleijadinho, who was born with deformed hands and limbs, rose above and beyond his physical shortcomings. Not only did he live independently for most of his life, he learned how to carve and whittle wood with nothing but a hammer and chisel tethered to his misshapen hands.

Soapstone was also liberally used in the churches of Minas Ferais for a number of reasons. Apart from its composition and longevity, the color of the talc-heavy rock, which came naturally in a pale oat with a greenish tinge, is said to never fade. Even better, soapstone is weather-resistant, and it does not expand or shrink in the heat. Soapstone tiles, which were crushed into triangular pieces, sanded down, and polished, when laid out in mosaic form, were also perfect for replicating the texture of skin from afar. Heitor would insist that it was he who first applied this intricate mosaic technique to a statue.

The soapstone the laborers would use to make the tiles were sourced from the quarries near Oura Preto, where Aleijadinho once worked, unaware of its limited supply. Heitor instructed the soapstone handlers to select the most immaculate stones in the creamiest colors; it was his intention to keep the original hue of the raw soapstone, so as to "reflect light from the sun, the moon, and surrounding spotlights." In doing so, even those gazing upon the monument from a distance, while unable to appreciate its sculptural details, would always see a flawless white cross. "I am fully enchanted with the result that you have achieved, and cannot but congratulate you on your idea [about using soapstone]," Landowski raved in another letter. "I fully share your opinion that this material will have a nobler and richer effect, in addition to being completely resistant to everything."

Meanwhile, Heitor kindled another partnership with a Romanian sculptor, Gheorghe Leonida, who would be responsible for crafting the face of the Redeemer. He had come highly recommended by Landowski. Entrusted with the responsibility of one of the monument's most salient focal points, the pressure was on for 33-year-old Leonida. With that said, this was nothing that he could not handle, for he was no stranger to pressure. Leonida had descended from a line of brilliant scientists, thinkers, and academics. His father, Dimitrie Leonida, was a celebrated inventor, and his older sister, Elisa, was a pioneer in her own right, said to be one of the world's first female engineers. Leonida, Jr., while just as well-read as his siblings and relatives, was more artistically inclined, and it was this passion in the arts that he chose to pursue. He brought even more glory to the Leonida name when his hauntingly sensual sculptures, "Reveil" (The Dream), and "Le Diable" (The Devil), received the grand prize at national art competitions held in Rome and Paris, respectively.

**The face of the statue**

The actual assembly of the Cristo Redentor would not begin until late 1926. The preparations and planning may have taken far longer than Heitor's crew had anticipated, but the chief engineer was on a stiflingly tight budget and literally could not afford to make any mistakes. With that established, in spite of all the delays, it seemed as if the team's perfectionism had paid off, for the laborers would have already been thoroughly well-versed on the execution of each of their roles, which streamlined the building process. By 1927, a temporary steel frame had already been planted onto the peak of Corcovado.

Women from all parishes volunteered as soapstone workers. Before and after service, women filed into the makeshift workshops set up in the back rooms of their churches. They formed an assembly line of sorts, gabbing animatedly amongst themselves as they stitched individual soapstone triangles – 3 centimeters long on all 3 sides, and about 5 mm thick – onto sheets of either mesh or linen cloth sprawled out across their work stations. Rumor has it that many of these women snuck tributes to their lovers, families, and friends on the back of the tiles before gluing them down to the mesh, effectively "sealing their love forever." Others chose to scratch prayers and quotes onto these tiles. A few carved their own names onto the triangles, infusing a little part of themselves into the statue forever. Lygia Maria Avila da Veiga, one of the soapstone workers, later reminisced with a twinkle in her eyes, "I wrote many wishes on the soapstones...They are up there, up there on top."

Heitor Levy was appointed the project manager, or "master builder" onsite, charged with supervising the progress and ensuring that everything was kept up to code. Veteran engineers Antonio Ferreira Antero and Pedro Fernandes Vianna da Silva were chosen to assist him.

Throughout the majority of the construction process, the entire monument, excluding the head of the Redeemer, was shrouded behind a complex network of wooden and metal scaffolding. Inside the hollow body of Christ was the frame Caquot had designed, skewered to the pedestal and secured to the terrace and earth underneath it. Massive concrete bricks, made out of dried clay, served as the bulk of the Redeemer's body and were carefully sunk into place. The molds used to create these bricks are said to have also been produced by Landowski. The builders stacked the bricks from the ground up, and the arms were only filled after reinforcement had been installed to support its weight. Last, but not least, the head of Christ completed the puzzle.

As well-organized and smooth-running as the process was, it was certainly grueling, arduous work. Laborers toiled under the sizzling sun and frigid rain, lugging concrete blocks from one place to another and stacking them for hours on end. Some operated the cog-wheel train nonstop, transporting beams and other heavy tools and equipment up and down the mountain. Mixing the cement was another thankless and taxing task, for the only source of water was a fountain that was about 1,000 feet away from the construction site. Most nerve-racking of all were the construction workers who balanced themselves on the wobbling beams of the scaffolding each day. Be that as it may, not a single soul was lost on the construction site – and if the stories are to be believed – there were no injuries, either.

This was not the only "miracle" associated with the Cristo Redentor. Heitor Levy, the project manager, was a devout Jew, and he found it deeply honorable to play such an integral role in its creation. He took the job most seriously, so much so that he flipped a farm that he owned in the area to make more room for the construction site. Upon the project's completion, he was so impressed by Christ's protection of the laborers that he soon converted to Catholicism. Another source, however, claims that it was when Levy suffered no injuries – not even the faintest scrape – from what would have otherwise been a fatal fall that he decided to change his stripes.

# History

**Ulysses R.J.'s panorama**

"For I know that my Redeemer lives, and that at the last He will stand upon the earth; and after my skin has been thus destroyed, then in my flesh I shall see God; whom I shall see on my side, and my eyes shall behold, and not another." – Job 19: 25-26

Construction of the Cristo Redentor finally wrapped up in early 1931, about 9 years after the first foundation stone was laid in April of 1922. It was officially unveiled before the public for the very first time on the 12th of October that year, and it was inaugurated via a celebratory Mass that same day. The ceremony had come just in time for the Nossa Senhora Aparecida, festivities devoted to "Our Lady of Aparacida," one of the many sobriquets dedicated to the Immaculate Conception, the Blessed Virgin Mary.

Though the construction had already been completed months beforehand, the opening day was postponed to make time for the preparations. A week before the snipping of the ceremonial ribbon, the Catholic Church convened in an ecclesiastical congress, where duties were allotted to all those present. Invitations, petitions, and necessary security permits were also taken care of during this time.

On the morning of opening day, the base of Mount Corcovado was swarming with tens of thousands of Brazilian Catholics and close to 500 priests from near and far. A wide selection of both local and foreign press came to photograph and document the historic event.

Brazilian President Getúlio Vargas, along with Cardinal Dom Sebastião Leme were selected to host the unveiling of the monument. Together, they delivered a poignant and well-rehearsed speech, wherein they dissected the definition of Christ as the Redeemer, explained the symbolic significance behind the statue, extolled the Catholic Church, and made a joint pledge to enhance the nation's evangelization program. Cardinal Leme, given the last word, chose to conclude his speech with the following message to the Brazilian people: "May this sacred image be the symbol of your place of life, of your protection, of your predilection, of your blessing which shines on Brazil and the Brazilians..."

After the speech and the blessing of the monument, which took place during the scheduled bell ringings of the city churches, the crowd reconvened for a "torch-lit retreat." But the celebrations did not end there; indeed, they spilled into the following week, which was dubbed "National Christ the Redeemer Week," during which more Brazilians from distant cities, as well as other visitors, traveled to Rio to marvel at the majestic monument.

Many of the infatuated visitors were supposedly stunned into silence as they laid eyes upon the Cristo Redentor for the very first time. It was a truly splendid sight indeed. The mighty figure of Christ, portrayed with his famous splayed arms, was perched upon a handsome octagonal pedestal. He seemed to look down upon them, his head ever-so-slightly bowed. Only those with near-perfect vision could make out the heart protruding from the Redeemer's partially exposed chest, as well as the crown of thorns that sat above his head, constructed out of lightning rods. Austrian writer Stefan Zweig captured the essence of the visitors' responses: "He seems to hold an immense cross over Rio and bless the city as a priest holding the monstrance over his faithful kneeling."

**Katia Lira's picture of the statue**

Aspiring and practicing boffins also pounced on the opportunity to use the inauguration of the Cristo Redentor as a stage for a groundbreaking experiment that married science with progress. The local triple threat, Francisco de Assis Chateaubriand, a politician, diplomat, and journalist, is said to have been the first to tender the idea. As outlined in his proposal, this was an attempt to illuminate the new monument from Naples, Italy. On paper, it sounded simple enough. From the transmission station in Naples, scientist Guglielmo Marconi would activate the illumination by sending a radio signal to Dorchester, England. Dorchester was then to relay this signal to the reception station in the Jacarepaguá district of Rio de Janeiro. Unfortunately, an untimely storm struck Naples that week, which jumbled up the signals, so at the end of the day, Brazilian authorities had no choice but to light up the monument manually.

To put into perspective just how much of an impact the monument would have on its people, one can examine the story of an unidentified sailor that transpired shortly after the opening of the monument. The sailor was cruising through Guanabara Bay when he detected some light bleeding out into the dark waters from the torch-lit procession by Mount Corcovado. Taking advantage of the clear view of the shore, he paddled towards the land, and parked it by the closest port. He disembarked from his ship and scanned his surroundings for the closest entertainment district, in search of a warm, hearty meal and bottomless pitchers of booze, which he hoped to enjoy with the town's loosest maidens. But as soon as he turned on his heel, he emitted a startled squeak, for above the sailor, who knew nothing about the monument, was a gargantuan image of Christ's unmistakable frame obscured by a tuft of clouds. Convinced that he had just been visited by the Savior, the trembling sailor staggered back to his ship. When he arrived back home, he immediately reached out to his local priest, unleashed upon the cleric decades' worth of confessions, and swore off cigarettes and booze for good.

All in all, the monument's bills rounded off to about $250,000, which is equivalent to roughly $3.2 million today. While this was anything but a negligible sum, experts maintain that this was a reasonable price, especially for a monument of such a size. The first blueprints revealed an estimate of the structure's dimensions: "Height: 30 meters (98.4 feet); Pedestal: 8 meters (26.2 feet);  Head: 3.75 meters (12.3 feet); Hand Length: 3.20 meters (10.5 feet); Distance fingertip to fingertip: 28 meters (92 feet)."

Evidently, the final product exceeded close to all expectations. The prodigious monument weighed a total of 1,145 tons (other sources claim it is closer to 1,400), with over 30 tons attributed to the head alone. The hefty arms weighed about 80 tons apiece, attached to hands that were 6 feet long (as large as the average adult male) and 8 tons each. The actual height of the monument, pedestal included, measured about 124-130 feet in height, and about 92-98 feet across. While the Cristo Redentor is not the largest statue of Christ, it is said to be the largest "art deco" statue in existence.

In contrast, the concrete interior of the monument was bland, dimly lit, and underwhelmingly decorated, reminiscent of a dusty, neglected warehouse. A half-paced stairwell took up most of the space in the interior, which created 12 "levels." The crisscrossing reinforced concrete beams that formed the internal structure of the monument served as levels, though floorless and mostly hollow save for a few narrow beams. On the 10th level, one would find two tunnel-like galleries extending from either side of the steps of the stairs, connected to five even narrower, inaccessible passages – these were of course, the arms and hands of the Redeemer. The 11th and 12th levels, on the other hand, were considerably more constricting in width, for this was the head of Christ.

The interior was completely sealed off, which robbed the space of natural light. Coupled with its thick, concrete walls, the maintenance workers and journalists – the only ones allowed inside of Christ – experience a bit of a draft, particularly during rainy days. They had only the illumination from a smattering of light bulbs, as well as the block numbers painted onto the walls of every level, to rely on.

The only attraction worth any interest in the monument's interior was found on the level of the Redeemer's breast. A short set of stairs leads to an outline of the protuberant "Sacred Heart of Jesus," measuring about 4.3 feet in height (1.30 meters), also laminated in tiny soapstone shells and flanked by dark gray lines resembling a rib cage. Legend has it that enclosed inside the sealed vessel of the sacred heart lies a small glass vial with a scroll of parchment inside of it, listing the names of Heitor Levy, his fiscal engineer, Pedro Fernandes Viana da Silva, and their families, meant not only to keep their descendants safe in the bosom of the Redeemer but as a "demonstration of their faith and gratitude."

Finally, on the righthand corner of the 10th level, one will find a small hatch. Maintenance workers squeeze themselves out of this secret trapdoor and onto the ledge outside of it – the right shoulder of the Redeemer – to perform routine checkups or reparations on the head, neck, chest, and other areas of Christ's upper body.  With a safety harness securely strapped around their own torsos, they are expected to carefully rappel themselves down from the shoulders to the bosom of Christ, using only their feet to maneuver themselves to the left hand side of the monument, if needed. To access the lower torso and legs of the Redeemer, the workers are made to crawl through the corridor-like passages of the arms.

The hollow pedestal, encrusted with gleaming granite slabs in midnight-black, was originally kept as such until 2006, when the Catholic Church established inside of it a charming modestly sized chapel consecrated to Our Lady of Aparedica, the Holy Protector of Brazil. The chapel itself, encompassed by plain white walls, measures about 26 feet in height and about 19.7 feet across. Like the pedestal, it is shaped like an octagon. Hovering above the glossy, smoky gray marble floors is a vaulted ceiling painted a periwinkle blue and outlined in white so as to mimic a clear, cloudless sky. The austerity of the chapel's built-in features offsets the fittings installed in it shortly thereafter. The chapel was furnished with six square lacquered wooden stools cushioned with red velvet, and a priest's chair, a baroque wooden throne with blood orange cushions. A small space between the stools was cleared for the aisle, which faced an elegant altar with a white marble countertop and matching charcoal-colored legs, adorned with fragrant bouquets. The wall behind the altar, which features a gold-plated tabernacle and a niche featuring the Lady's tunic as its centerpiece, was dressed up with the same periwinkle blue and a mist of fluffy white clouds, an illusory extension of the ceiling in the sky.

The chapel was not the only recent installment. Three years before its doors were opened, elevators, escalators, and brand-new walkways were added to the compound.

Heitor was positive that the monument, made impregnable by its precise calculations and flawless design – including the ability to withstand winds of over 155 miles per hour (250 kilometers per hour) – was indestructible. But as is usually the case with just about any monument displayed outdoors, it would only be a matter of time before Mother Nature took its toll on the Cristo Redentor. Around 1939, a mere eight years after the monument's completion, damage to the statue first became visible.

Heitor himself was fully aware of the perils that would arise from fixing a monument onto a peak over 2,300 feet above ground. This was why the crown of lightning rods atop the Redeemer's head was built in the first place. Sadly, the lightning rods, which snaked all the way down the sides of Christ's arms, could only do so much to stave off the fiery bolts of electricity that rained from above on the stormiest of nights. In fact, Brazil was among the top "lightning capitals" on the planet. Based on statistics provided by the Brazilian Institute of Space Research, the Cristo Redentor is struck by an average of 2 to 4 "direct hits" each year. For the first 50 or 60 years, the monument sustained only minor injuries, such as the chipping of a soapstone tile from a wayward bolt of lightning. But in recent years, Brazil has been plagued by progressively violent hurricanes, the most severe of which has overwhelmed the monument's lightning rods. One superstorm managed to blast off the Redeemer's middle fingertip and left glaring streaks of burn marks on the back of Christ's head. All this damage would cost the Church, too. The bill for the repairs on the damage caused by the lightning strikes in January of 2014 alone came to a staggering total of 1.9 million reals (about $568,537 USD). Said Dr. Osmar Pinto, who presides over the atmospheric electric group of the BISR, "In the past few years, there have been some cases of storms registering more than 1,000 lightning bolts, which did not occur previously...[This is why] it is necessary to review the structure of the statue periodically, and revise the earthing system of the lightning rods."

In early 2015, workers were ordered to prolong the lightning rods so that it ended not at the cuffs of Christ's robe but at the fingertips, while the rest of the maintenance crew simultaneously earthed the new rods (the action of linking the lightning rods to the ground). Perfecting the technique of effectively earthing these rods would take some time and effort in itself, as granite is known to be a poor conductor of electricity.

The rapidly dwindling supply of gray-green soapstone is yet another stumbling block that has recently presented itself to renovators. As such, certain patches of the monument that have been retouched are growing increasingly darker with time, with shades that leaned closer to a cloudy gray with some bluish-green luster. According to Marcia Braga, who oversaw the 2010 renovations, which included the substitution of close to 60,000 soapstone triangles, she had no choice but to reject more than 80% of the samples supplied to her by the quarry. Bearing this in mind, Braga and other experts maintain that rumors that authorities are contemplating the replacement of all 6 million-plus tiles are unfounded.

On top of these hassles, the Cristo Redentor continues to be harassed by another recurring dilemma: vandalism. The first known case was reported in 1991, when an unnamed gang of graffiti artists tagged the base with spray paint. But it was one case, which came 19 years later, that took the nation by storm. One evening in mid-April of 2010, 28-year-old Paulo Souza dos Santos, an ex-military man, marched into his local police station, his head hung low with shame. He was there to turn himself in. The previous night, Santos, along with his accomplice, 26-year-old Edmar Batista de Carvalho, slipped past security and shimmied up to the shoulder of the Redeemer, where they then proceeded to spray-paint the head, chest, and arms of Christ.

Initially, the pair were facing a 3-year prison sentence, for they were potentially guilty of two grievous offenses: inflicting "discriminatory injury" on a religious image and desecrating environmental property (since Corcovado was enclosed within Tijuca Naitonal Park). Only when the remorseful duo agreed to issue a groveling apology to "God and the Rio population" was the sentence revoked. The alarming messages, which included alarming phrases such as "React Rio!" and the age-old taunt "When the cat's away, the mice will play" to protest the authorities' inaction on a string of missing persons cases, were hosed off by a professional cleaning crew the day after the incident, and the vandals were made to scrub off the graffiti on the walls of a nearby tunnel as punishment.

Despite all the precautions taken by authorities, the ongoing problem of vandalism has yet to see a decline. Just a few years after the sensational case of Santos and Carvalho, rabid Atletico-MG fan, Michael Antonio Silva Azevedo, was caught tagging the back of the Cristo Redentor with a sloppy homage to his all-time favorite player, Ronaldinho. Eduardo Paes, then the mayor of Rio de Janeiro, estimates that the city spends at least $300,000 reals ($150,000) each year on graffiti-cleaning alone.

In July of 2007, the Cristo Redentor was officially crowned one of the "New" Seven Wonders of the World. While the cynical have likened the monument to no more than a tourist trap, it continues to be of momentous importance not only to the Brazilian Catholics but the enthusiastic 2 million-plus visitors the statue receives each year.

In 2011, Peter Gasper, a specialist in "plastic art," was hired to outfit the monument with 300 energy-efficient LED projector bulbs. These bulbs, to be lit up on special occasions, were hooked up to a system that allowed the operator to change the colors, as well as control the speed and intensity of the lights. On Mother's Day, for instance, one will find the monument bathed in a gentle, soothing lilac. On Autism Awareness Day, the Cristo Redentor turns a cool, blue shade.

**Shana Reis' picture of the statue lit up in November 2015**

Today, Mount Corcovado hosts a lively, flamboyant street party known as the "Suvaco do Cristo," or "Christ's Armpit," each year, during the nation's pre-Lent Carnival. Crowds consisting of hundreds upon hundreds of effervescent locals (mostly youths clad in T-shirts with the face of Christ printed onto them), vivacious dancers, and samba musicians, parade around the blessed mountain, serenading the Cristo Redentor.

Brazil's Christ the Redeemer statue is undoubtedly the most identifiable Christian monument in the Latin world, but part of its splendor lies in all the different interpretations of the Cristo Redentor. This is more than just a "monument to science, art, and religion" – some say it is an act of rebellion against secularism. As Nora Heimann, the chairwoman of Catholic University's Art Department, put it, "This is a triumphant image. Most people describe it as a sort of globalization of Christ crucified." To the non-religious, who cite the monument's outstretched arms, the statue is a symbol of welcome.

Whatever the monument symbolizes, it cannot be denied that the Cristo Redentor is an indispensable part of the nation's rich and riveting history.

### Online Resources

Other books about Christ the Redeemer on Amazon

### Further Reading

Bromley, D. G. (2014, April 28). Christ the Redeemer. Retrieved
December 12, 2017, from https://wrldrels.org/2016/10/08/christ-the-
redeemer/

Bowater, D., Mulvey, S., & Misra, T. (2014, March 10). Arms wide open.
Retrieved December 12, 2017, from
http://www.bbc.com/news/special/2014/newsspec_7141/index.html

Craven, J. (2017, March 30). 5 Reasons Why We Care About Cristo
Redentor. Retrieved December 12, 2017, from
https://www.thoughtco.com/reasons-why-christ-the-redeemer-statue-is-so-
popular-4123653

Editors, D. (2012, September 11). Christ the Redeemer: 10 things you did
not know. Retrieved December 12, 2017, from
http://www.daytours4u.com/en/rdj4u/christ-the-redeemer-10-things-you-did-
not-know/

Brown, S. (2017, January 31). A History of Rio de Janeiro's Christ the
Redeemer Monument. Retrieved December 12, 2017, from
https://theculturetrip.com/south-america/brazil/articles/a-history-of-the-
christ-the-redeemer-monument/

Rodriguez, J. (2017, November 12). Construction Facts About Brazil's
Christ the Redeemer. Retrieved December 12, 2017, from
https://www.thebalance.com/christ-the-redeemer-construction-facts-844362

Editors, V. H. (2016). 19 Awesome and Interesting Facts About Christ the
Redeemer Statue. Retrieved December 12, 2017, from
https://vacayholics.com/interesting-facts-about-christ-redeemer-statue

Wells, J. (2016, August 11). 11 Facts About Rio's Christ the Redeemer
Statue. Retrieved December 12, 2017, from
http://mentalfloss.com/article/84546/11-facts-about-rios-christ-redeemer-
statue

Editors, S. D. (2009, August). Christ the Redeemer, Rio de Janeiro.
Retrieved December 12, 2017, from http://www.sacred-
destinations.com/brazil/rio-christ-the-redeemer

Editors, S. S. (2015). The Design and Construction of 'Christ the

Redeemer'. Retrieved December 12, 2017, from http://thesevensistersseries.com/christ-the-redeemer/4592929034

Editors, C. (2011). Curiosities. Retrieved December 12, 2017, from https://en.cristoredentoroficial.com.br/curiosidades

Cernat, O. (2015, August 25). Povestea enigmaticului sculptor român care a cioplit chipul lui Iisus din Rio de Janeiro. Statuia este şi acum cel mai mare simbol al creştinismului din lume. Retrieved December 12, 2017, from http://adevarul.ro/locale/galati/povestea-enigmaticului-sculptor-roman-cioplit-chipul-iisus-rio-janeiro-statuia-mai-mare-simbol-crestinismului-lume-1_55db09baf5eaafab2cde992b/index.html

McMahon, M. (2017, December 6). What is Christ the Redeemer? Retrieved December 12, 2017, from http://www.wisegeek.com/what-is-christ-the-redeemer.htm

Boorstein, M. (2016, August 9). The many meanings of Rio's massive Christ statue. Retrieved December 12, 2017, from https://www.washingtonpost.com/news/acts-of-faith/wp/2016/08/09/the-many-meanings-of-rios-massive-christ-statue/?utm_term=.a4c01c2d6e57

Editors, C. M. (2013, December 7). St. Ambrose, the Honey Tongued Doctor. Retrieved December 12, 2017, from http://catholicmajority.com/st-ambrose/

Dawson, R. (2014, May 20). Brazil: Where God is on the pitch. Retrieved December 12, 2017, from http://www.bbc.co.uk/religion/0/27379992

Araujo, M. (2011). Is Christ the Redeemer statue in Rio de Janeiro lit up at night? Retrieved December 12, 2017, from http://www.myriotravelguide.com/is-christ-the-redeemer-statue-in-rio-de-janeiro-lit-up-at-night/

Tickle, G. (2015, December 31). Urban Explorers Climb the Massive Christ the Redeemer Statue in Rio de Janeiro During the Night. Retrieved December 12, 2017, from https://laughingsquid.com/urban-explorers-climb-the-massive-christ-the-redeemer-statue-in-rio-de-janeiro-during-the-night/

Clayton, J. (2015, December 14). Watch: Urban Explorers Climb Rio de Janeiro's Christ The Redeemer Statue At Night. Retrieved December 12,

2017, from https://mpora.com/travel/watch-urban-explorers-climb-rio-de-janeiros-christ-the-redeemer-statue-at-night#ifsOrYIaJS4qhiJD.97

Edney, L. (2012, March 27). A Visit to Christ the Redeemer in Rio. Retrieved December 12, 2017, from http://riotimesonline.com/brazil-news/rio-travel/a-visit-to-christ-the-redeemer-in-rio/

Editors, L. P. (2014). Parque Nacional da Tijuca. Retrieved December 12, 2017, from https://www.lonelyplanet.com/brazil/rio-de-janeiro/attractions/parque-nacional-da-tijuca/a/poi-sig/1269053/363153

Editors, B. C. (2012, July 17). God is Brazilian - The Story of Christo Redentor. Retrieved December 13, 2017, from http://www.brazil-compass.com/2012/07/god-is-brazilian-story-of-christo.html

Editors, R. G. (2011). Corcovado Mountain & Christ the Redeemer. Retrieved December 13, 2017, from http://www.rioguides.com/us/information/rio-s-attractions/the-obvious/18-corcovado-mountain-christ-the-redeemer-us

Editors, H. D. (2013). The Catholic Church in Brazil. Retrieved December 13, 2017, from https://rlp.hds.harvard.edu/faq/catholic-church-brazil

Editors, N. A. (2011). Brazil. Retrieved December 13, 2017, from http://www.newadvent.org/cathen/02745c.htm

Novais, A. (2013, January 8). All About Religions in Brazil. Retrieved December 13, 2017, from http://thebrazilbusiness.com/article/all-about-religions-in-brazil

Editors, C. S. (2012). Brazil - Roman Catholicism. Retrieved December 13, 2017, from http://countrystudies.us/brazil/42.htm

Editors, R. G. (2015). Corcovado. Retrieved December 13, 2017, from https://riotheguide.com/corcovado-2/

Luiz, A. (2011, October 12). O Corcovado - Padre Pedro Maria Boss, missionário lazarista. Retrieved December 13, 2017, from https://www.gloria.tv/article/RzjyTacXkCyS4d1gABbjf8gsG

Editors, E. (2014). Isabel of Brazil (1846–1921). Retrieved December 13, 2017, from http://www.encyclopedia.com/women/encyclopedias-almanacs-transcripts-and-maps/isabel-brazil-1846-1921

Serbin, K. P. (2012). Needs of the Heart: A Social and Cultural History of Brazil's Clergy and Seminaries. Retrieved December 13, 2017, from https://muse.jhu.edu/article/501233/summary

Schulze, F. (2015, March 16). Brazil. Retrieved December 13, 2017, from https://encyclopedia.1914-1918-online.net/article/brazil

Tavener, B. (2014, November 9). Brazil: The only Latin American nation to fight in World War I. Retrieved December 13, 2017, from https://bentavener.com/2014/11/09/brazil-the-only-latin-nation-to-fight-in-world-war-i/

Green, J. N. (2004). Rio de Janeiro - GLBTQ. Retrieved December 13, 2017, from http://www.glbtqarchive.com/ssh/rio_de_janeiro_S.pdf

Editors, L. C. (2006, September 8). 1917-1918: The Brazilian anarchist uprising. Retrieved December 14, 2017, from https://libcom.org/history/1918-brazilian-anarchist-uprising

Trueman, C. N. (2015, April 17). First World War Casualties. Retrieved December 14, 2017, from http://www.historylearningsite.co.uk/world-war-one/world-war-one-and-casualties/first-world-war-casualties/

Da Costa Goulart, A. (2005, April). Revisiting the Spanish flu: the 1918 influenza pandemic in Rio de Janeiro1. Retrieved December 14, 2017, from http://www.scielo.br/scielo.php?pid=S0104-59702005000100006&script=sci_arttext&tlng=en

Editors, L. P. (2015). Chances of seeing monkeys and other wildlife in Tijuca? Retrieved December 14, 2017, from https://www.lonelyplanet.com/thorntree/forums/americas-south-america/brazil/chances-of-seeing-monkeys-and-other-wildlife-in-tijuca

Neffinger, V. (2016, August 12). What is the Significance of Rio's Christ the Redeemer Statue? Retrieved December 14, 2017, from https://www.christianheadlines.com/blog/what-is-the-significance-of-rio-s-christ-the-redeemer-statue.html

Editors, B. (2013, March 14). How many Roman Catholics are there in the world? Retrieved December 14, 2017, from http://www.bbc.com/news/world-21443313

Meyer, A. (2010). Portuguese Colonisation Of Brazil. Retrieved December 14, 2017, from http://www.brazil.org.za/portuguese-colonisation-of-brazil.html

Editors, H. W. (2011). HISTORY OF BRAZIL . Retrieved December 14, 2017, from http://www.historyworld.net/wrldhis/PlainTextHistories.asp?historyid=aa88

Editors, S. S. (2015, July 1). Brazilwood – What would Brazil be without it? Retrieved December 14, 2017, from https://streetsmartbrazil.com/brazilwood-what-would-brazil-be-without-it/

Manthrone, K. (2017, July 21). FEMALE EYES ON SOUTH AMERICA: MARIA GRAHAM. Retrieved December 14, 2017, from http://www.coleccioncisneros.org/editorial/cite-site-sights/female-eyes-south-america-maria-graham

Editors, F. L. (2007). State and race in the Brazilian Empire. Retrieved December 14, 2017, from https://www.thefreelibrary.com/State and race in the Brazilian Empire-a0191817962

Editors, I. (2007, January 13). Christ the Redeemer as a Sacred Place. Retrieved December 14, 2017, from http://iguassufallsareatips.blogspot.tw/2007/01/christ-redeemer-as-sacred-place.html

Editors, D. D. (2017, October 9). DIARIO DO CORCOVADO FOTOS PROFISSIONAIS NO CRISTO REDENTOR E RIO DE JANEIRO INFORMAÇÕES TURÍSTICAS. Retrieved December 14, 2017, from https://diariodocorcovado.blogspot.tw/2017/10/diario-do-corcovadso-especial.html

Editors, S. W. (2012). Heitor da Silva Costa. Retrieved December 14, 2017, from http://www.wonders-of-the-world.net/Christ-the-Redeemer/Heitor-da-Silva-Costa.php

Editors, S. W. (2011). Christ the Redeemer at Rio. Retrieved December 14, 2017, from http://wwww.wonders-of-the-world.net/Christ-the-Redeemer/index.php

Editors, C. I. (2015, October 4). Christ the Redeemer, Paul Landowski. Retrieved December 14, 2017, from https://www.google.com/culturalinstitute/beta/exhibit/zgKCuAa4ZltQLQ

Riley, L. (2014). Paul Landowski. Retrieved December 14, 2017, from http://thesevensistersseries.com/paul-landowski/4586903625

Editors, N. T. (1976, November 30). ALBERT CAQUOT. Retrieved December 14, 2017, from http://www.nytimes.com/1976/11/30/archives/albert-caquot.html

Editors, R. (2017, September 19). Albert Caquot. Retrieved December 14, 2017, from https://www.revolvy.com/main/index.php?s=Albert%20Caquot&item_type=topic

Editors, A. C. (2012, March 11). Gheorghe Leonida – Romanian contribution to "Cristo Redentor". Retrieved December 14, 2017, from https://anothercoolro.wordpress.com/2012/03/11/gheorghe-leonida-romanian-contribution-to-cristo-redentor/

Zeldenrust, J. W. (2017, November 27). 8 must-know facts before visiting Christ the Redeemer in Rio de Janeiro. Retrieved December 14, 2017, from http://www.gringo-rio.com/facts-christ-the-redeemer-rio-de-janeiro/

Editors, B. (2013). Revista Feminina, 1935, ano XXIII, n 259. Retrieved December 14, 2017, from https://bibdig.biblioteca.unesp.br/handle/10/6339

Martins, L. B. (2017, June 5). Uma questão de fé. Retrieved December 14, 2017, from https://vejario.abril.com.br/cidades/fotos-cristo-2/

Editors, O. M. (2007, June 29). RIO DE JANEIRO QUER A SÉTIMA MARAVILHA. Retrieved December 14, 2017, from http://www.overmundo.com.br/banco/rio-de-janeiro-quer-a-setima-maravilha

De Lima, L. (2011, June 10). Em escritura registrada em cartório, autor do projeto do Cristo cedeu à Igreja os direitos autorais da obra. Retrieved December 15, 2017, from https://oglobo.globo.com/rio/em-escritura-registrada-em-cartorio-autor-do-projeto-do-cristo-cedeu-igreja-os-direitos-autorais-da-obra-2865762

Editors, T. (1942, October 26). Milestones, Oct. 26, 1942. Retrieved

December 15, 2017, from
http://content.time.com/time/magazine/article/0,9171,850165,00.html

Editors, T. (1930, November 3). BRAZIL: Where is the President?
Retrieved December 15, 2017, from
http://content.time.com/time/magazine/article/0,9171,882373-2,00.html

Editors, N. A. (2017). Eucharistic Congresses. Retrieved December 15,
2017, from http://www.newadvent.org/cathen/05592a.htm

Editors, R. (2017, November 23). Epitácio da Silva Pessoa. Retrieved
December 15, 2017, from https://www.revolvy.com/main/index.php?
s=Epit%C3%A1cio%20da%20Silva%20Pessoa&item_type=topic

Cline, A. (2017, July 23). Second Commandment: Thou Shalt Not Make
Graven Images. Retrieved December 15, 2017, from
https://www.thoughtco.com/second-commandment-thou-shalt-not-make-
graven-images-250901

Oakes, J. (2012, January 30). Why do Protestants object to crucifixes?
Retrieved December 15, 2017, from http://evidenceforchristianity.org/why-
do-protestants-object-to-crucifixes/

Editors, A. (2009). Paul Landowski - A Humanist Artist. Retrieved
December 15, 2017, from
http://www.angelfire.com/scifi2/rsolecki/images/Landowski_photo1.htm

Editors, W. W. (2012). Construction of Christ the Redeemer. Retrieved
December 15, 2017, from http://www.wonders-of-the-world.net/Christ-the-
Redeemer/Construction-of-Christ-the-Redeemer.php

Editors, F. W. (2017, April 11). Gentil & Bourdet. Retrieved December 15,
2017, from https://fr.wikipedia.org/wiki/Gentil_%26_Bourdet

Editors, E. B. (2011, September 16). Aleijadinho. Retrieved December 15,
2017, from https://www.britannica.com/biography/Aleijadinho

Editors, R. H. (2014). CHRIST THE REDEEMER: GET TO KNOW THE
HISTORY OF THIS WONDER OF THE MODERN WORLD. Retrieved
December 15, 2017, from https://rederiohoteis.com/en/christ-the-redeemer-
get-to-know-the-history-of-this-wonder-of-the-modern-world/

Editors, W. W. (2011). Inauguration of Christ the Redeemer. Retrieved December 15, 2017, from http://www.wonders-of-the-world.net/Christ-the-Redeemer/Inauguration-of-Christ-the-Redeemer.php

Editors, W. W. (2011). Description of Christ the Redeemer. Retrieved December 15, 2017, from http://www.wonders-of-the-world.net/Christ-the-Redeemer/Description-of-Christ-the-Redeemer.php

Editors, W. W. (2011). The chapel of Our Lady of Aparecida. Retrieved December 15, 2017, from http://www.wonders-of-the-world.net/Christ-the-Redeemer/Chapel-our-Lady-of-Aparecida.php

Editors, L. (2010, April 14). Suspect in Vandalism of Iconic Brazilian Monument Surrenders. Retrieved December 15, 2017, from http://www.laht.com/article.asp?articleid=355823&categoryid=14090

Newman, B. (2012, June 13). 'Christ the Redeemer' gets a Ronaldinho graffiti makeover, but the vandal makes a stupid spelling error. Retrieved December 15, 2017, from https://www.101greatgoals.com/blog/christ-redeemer-gets-ronaldinho-graffiti-makeover-vandal-makes-stupid-spelling-error/

Ebright, O. (2009, October 20). Brazilians Offended Over Destruction of Christ the Redeemer. Retrieved December 15, 2017, from https://www.nbclosangeles.com/news/local/2012-Movie-Billboard-La-Brea-65011882.html